Helping Hands

At the Animal Hospital

Ruth Thomson

WAYLAND

First published in 2006 by Wayland,
an imprint of Hachette Children's Books

Reprinted in 2007

This paperback edition published in 2008 by Wayland,
an imprint of Hachette Children's Books

Copyright © Wayland 2006

Editor: Laura Milne
Managing Editor: Victoria Brooker
Senior Design Manager: Rosamund Saunders

Design: Proof Books
Commissioned photography: Chris Fairclough

British Library Cataloguing in Publication Data:

Thomson, Ruth
Helping hands at the animal hospital
1. Veterinary hospitals – Juvenile literature
2. Veterinarians – Juvenile literature
I. Title II. At the animal hospital
636'.089

ISBN: 978-0-7502-5609-4

Printed and bound in China

Wayland
338 Euston Road, London NW1 3BH

Acknowledgements
The author and publisher would like to thank the following
people for their help and participation in this book:
Alan Krasno, Maria Mighall, Andrew Parry, Toni Vivian,
Nicola Tarrant, Ruth Miles, Lydia Shilling, Julia Withers
and Erin Brickell at The Barn Animal Hospital, Old Basing;
Shelagh Krasno, Alice Krasno, Katie Swinton-Clark,
G. Swinton-Clark, E.A. Skeggs, Edward Hodgson, George
Hodgson, Anne Morris, Emily Morris, Chloe McLowskey, Vicki
Nicholas, Jenny Faulkner-Quick, Wendy MacLennan, Ruth
Miles, Zoe Clifford, Kristy Willis, V. Cornwall, Aprille Ager,
Charlotte Ager.

Contents

Words printed in **bold** are explained in the glossary.

The team

We work at an animal hospital. Four **vets**, eight **veterinary nurses** and a secretary work here. We look after ill or injured animals. We also examine animals to make sure they stay healthy.

▲ Bertie, the hospital cat

▼ Our team at the animal hospital

We mainly look after cats, dogs, rabbits and guinea pigs. We have also seen unusual animals such as a python, an iguana, a monkey and a swan.

When to take your pet to the vet

* Once a year for a check-up and **vaccinations.**
* If it stops eating and drinking.
* If it keeps scratching.
* If it keeps sneezing or coughing.
* If it is hurt or limping.
* If it has an eye or ear infection.

◄ This girl and her mother are bringing their pet guinea pig to see us.

7

At reception

We are **veterinary nurses** who help look after the animals. We also work at **reception**.

▲ We welcome people and their pets when they arrive.

◄ People call us to make **appointments**.

We often give people advice about their pets. ▶

The **pharmacy** stocks creams, powders, pills and sprays. A **vet** types out a **prescription** for a medicine and I find the right bottle.

▼ I label the bottle of medicine.

The waiting room

People wait with their pets to see a **vet**. They can read our newsletter. They can look on a noticeboard which shows animals that need new homes.

Owners can buy dog and cat food, collars, leads and toys for their pets. ▶

▼ Pets and their owners wait to see a vet.

Whilst they are waiting, children can draw a picture of their favourite animal. We pin the pictures on to a noticeboard for everyone to see.

▼ Children can sit at a desk with paper, crayons and coloured pens.

How to keep your cat or dog healthy

* Give it fresh food twice a day – but do not overfeed.
* Make sure it has clean water all day.
* Make sure its bedding is clean.
* Groom it regularly.
* Vaccinate and worm it against disease.
* Take a dog for a walk twice a day.

A cat check-up

I am the chief **vet**. I see animals in my consulting room. My first visitor today is Frostie.

I listen to Frostie's heart and lungs with my **stethoscope**. ▶

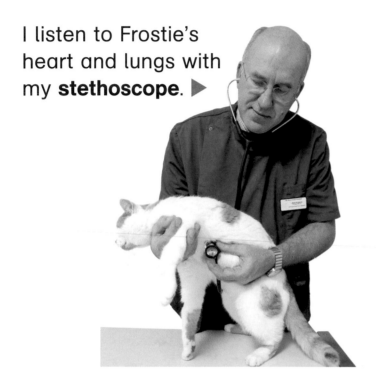

How to tell if a cat is healthy

* It has a glossy coat and bushy tail.
* It has a moist nose and glistening eyes.
* It wants food regularly.
* It purrs when you stroke it.
* It likes to play.

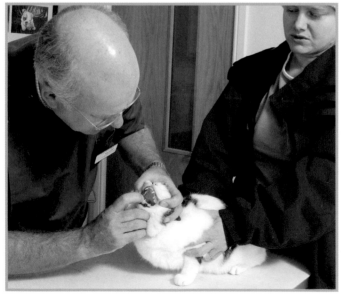

▲ I check Frostie's teeth.

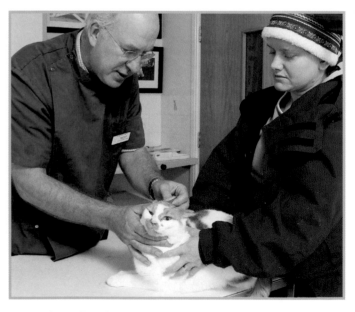

▲ I look down her ears to make sure they are clean.

I have special tools for different jobs. Here are some of them.

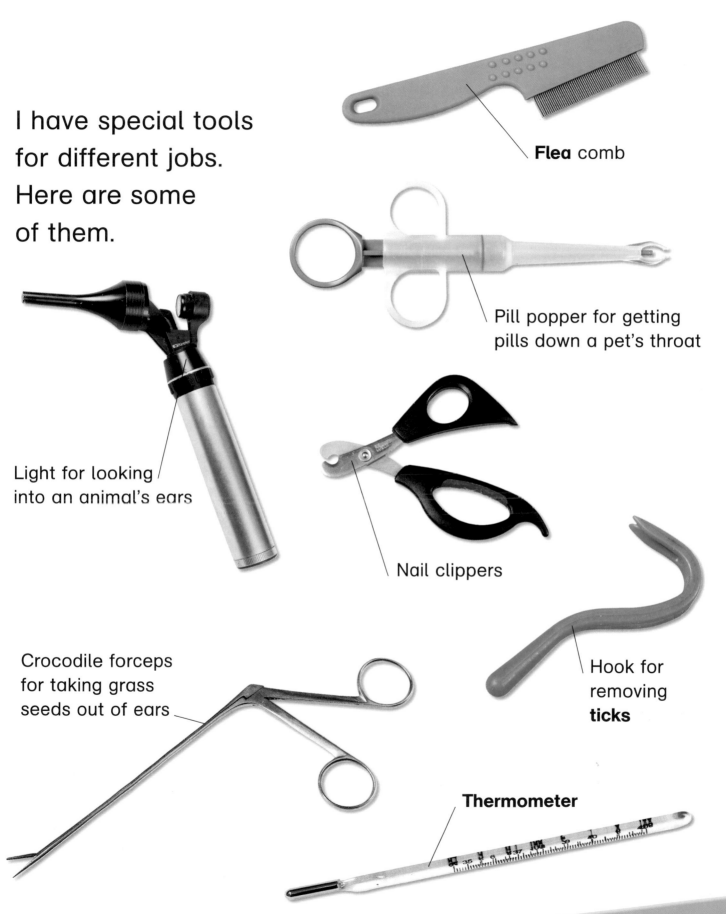

Flea comb

Pill popper for getting pills down a pet's throat

Light for looking into an animal's ears

Nail clippers

Hook for removing **ticks**

Crocodile forceps for taking grass seeds out of ears

Thermometer

13

Kittens and puppies

When kittens and puppies are eight weeks old, their owners bring them for their first **vaccinations**.

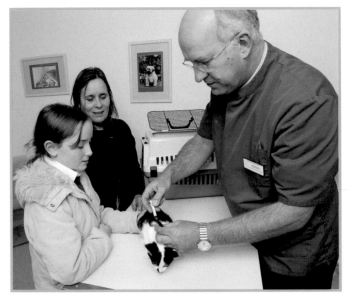

▲ I inject the vaccination into the soft spot of Honeymae's neck.

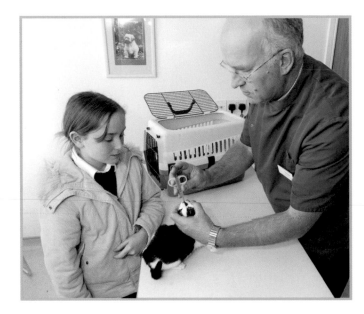

▲ I give her a worming pill.

I write down the date and details in her vaccine book. ▶

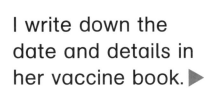

I ask owners if their pets have been coughing or sneezing or had any tummy upsets.

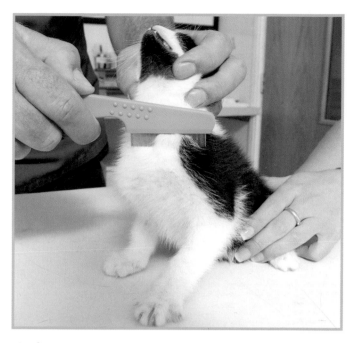

▲ I run a comb through Topsy's fur to check for **fleas**.

Humphrey sits in the scales to be weighed. ▶

Treating animals

Pets come here for all sorts of reasons.
If a pet has a sore throat and a cough, I will take their **temperature** with a **thermometer**.

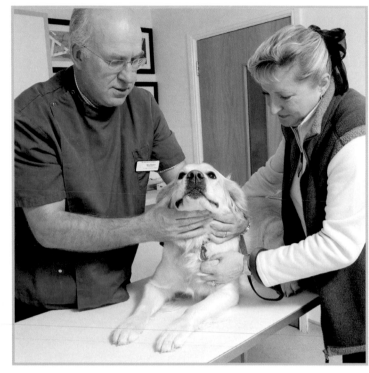

I feel under Elsa's neck to see if it is swollen. ▶

▼ I weigh Midge the guinea pig to check that she is eating enough.

Sometimes we inject a tiny microchip under the skin of a dog or cat in case it goes missing, or if the pet is going abroad.

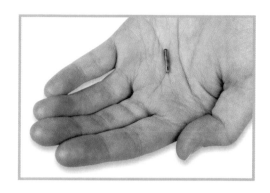

▲ The tiny microchip has a number just for that animal.

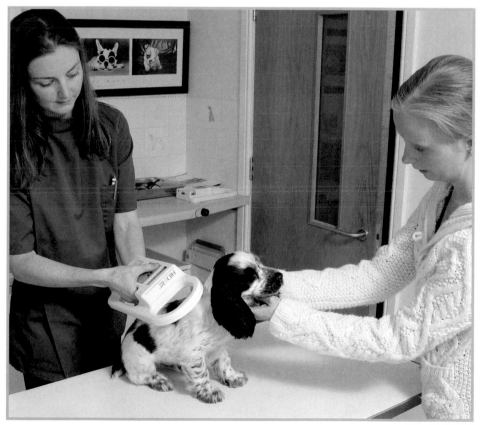

▲ I check that a microchip reader can read the microchip.

Pets need their own passport if they are going abroad. ▶

A closer look

We cannot always tell what is wrong with animals just by looking at them. We need to find out in other ways.

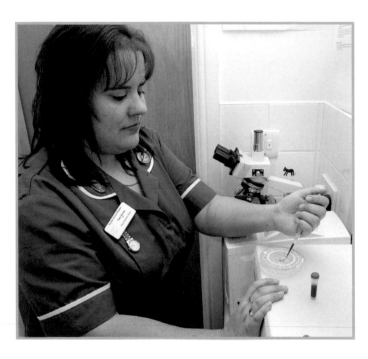

I test an animal's blood in a machine to see what is wrong. ▶

I take an **x-ray** if I think an animal has a broken bone. ▼

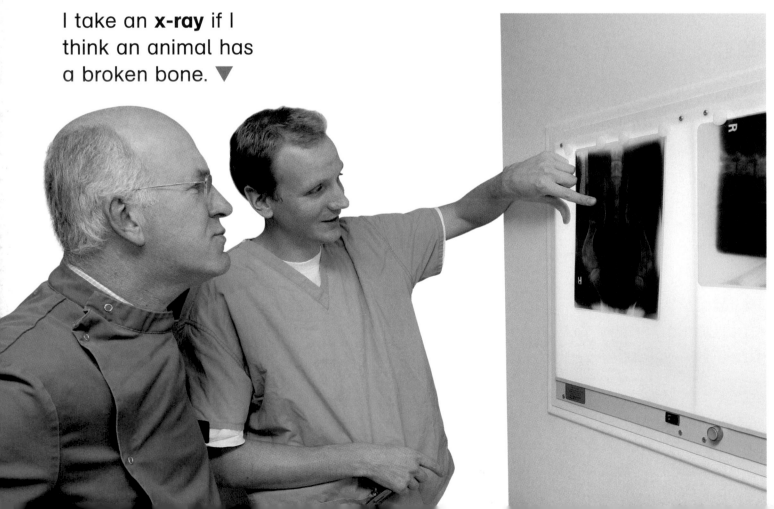

Sometimes we scan an animal. This gives us a picture of the animal's insides on a computer screen. The picture may show what is wrong with the animal.

▼ I move the scanner over a cat's tummy.

The operating theatre

Operations are done in a very clean room called an operating theatre. I put on a **sterile** gown and make sure my hands are clean. Then I put on thin rubber gloves.

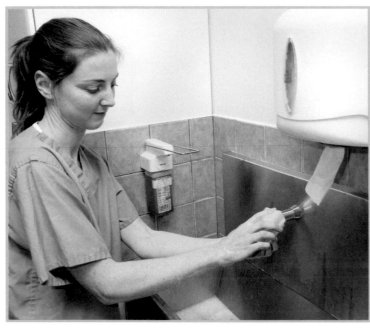

▲ I wash my hands very well.

Fifi has an **anaesthetic** to send her to sleep, so she will not feel any pain. ▶

A nurse helps me prepare Fifi for an operation.

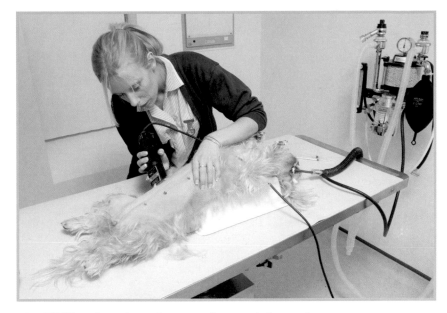

▲ Fifi's fur is shaved and her bare skin cleaned.

▼ I cover Fifi with a drape, unwrap my surgical tools and do the operation.

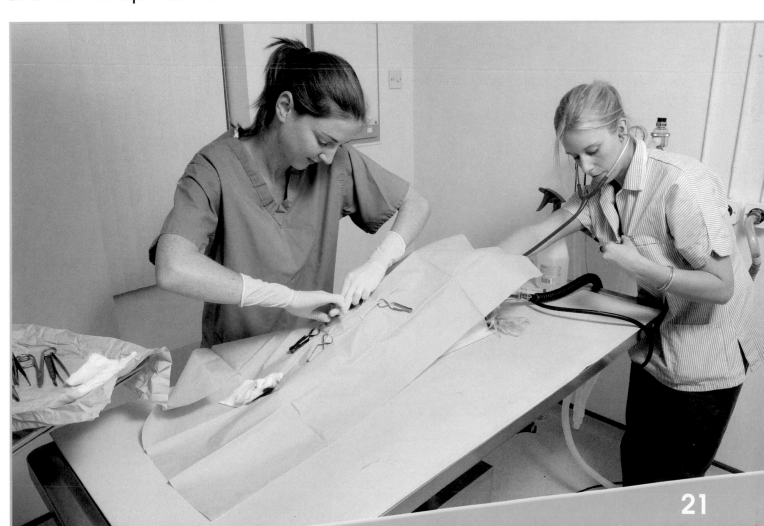

Animals that stay

Animals sometimes stay for more treatment – either just for the day, overnight or for several days. The animals each have a cage of their own. They rest there before and after an **operation**.

▼ Fifi has woken up and is ready to eat.

I am a kennel girl.
I clean the cages
and put down clean
newspaper and a
soft mat. I give the
animals fresh water.

▲ Cleaning out a cage

I walk the dogs
in the garden once
they have recovered
from an operation. ▶

Veterinary nurses

We help to look after the animals. We work in **shifts**, so there is always someone here day and night. In the morning, we check on animals that have stayed overnight.

◀ I check that every animal has the right food and medicine.

We also help the **vet** in the surgery. I help the vet file and smooth a rabbit's teeth.

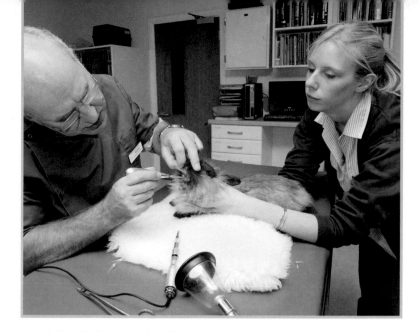

▲ I hold a rabbit to keep him still.

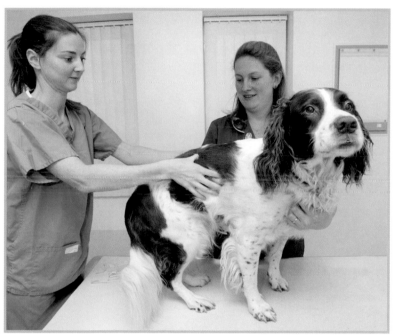

◀ Murphy has sore legs. I hold him while the vet finds out where it hurts.

I hold Murphy while the vet puts in **acupuncture** needles to lessen the pain. ▶

Home visits

Some animals are too big or too ill to travel easily to the hospital, so I visit them at home. Today I am going to visit a dog and a horse.

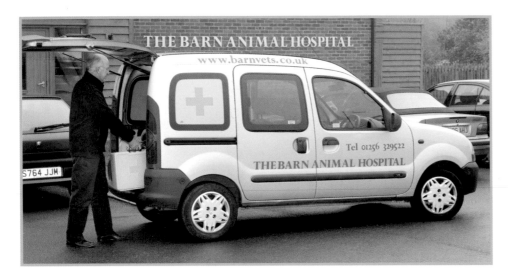

◀ I drive the hospital ambulance, taking my medical kit with me.

Harry has cut his leg and cannot walk very well. I change his dressing. ▶

I look at Ginger Pop's eyes to make sure they have cleared up properly after an infection. ▶

◀ I examine her feet to make sure they are healthy.

Glossary

acupuncture a method of treating animals (and people) by pricking the skin with needles

anaesthetic a drug that puts an animal (or person) deeply to sleep before an operation

appointment a time and a place when people meet

flea a tiny jumping insect that can live on animals and bite them

operation something done by a vet (or surgeon) to repair or remove part of an animal's (or person's) body

pharmacy a shop selling medicines

prescription a note written by a vet (or a doctor) that says what medicine a patient needs

reception the place where people check in and make appointments

shift a period of time that someone does his or her work

stethoscope an instrument that vets (and doctors) use to listen to the heart and lungs

sterile completely clean and free of germs

temperature how hot or cold something is

thermometer an instrument that measures how hot or cold something is

tick a small insect that burrows into an animal's skin and sucks its blood

vaccination putting medicine into an animal's (or person's) blood to stop them from catching a disease

vet short for veterinary surgeon, someone who treats and prevents illnesses in animals

veterinary nurse a nurse who has been trained to look after sick or injured animals

x-ray a photograph of the inside of the body

Quiz

Look back through the book to do this quiz.

1 How often should you take your pet to see a vet?

2 How can you tell if a cat is healthy?

3 What is a prescription?

4 Why does a vet take an x-ray?

5 How does a vet check whether a cat has fleas?

6 How does a vet take an animal's temperature?

7 What is an anaesthetic?

8 Where do animals stay before an operation?

Answers

1 Once a year.

2 A healthy cat has a glossy coat, bushy tail, moist nose and glistening eyes. It will want food regularly, purrs when you stroke it, and want to play.

3 A note written by a vet that says what medicine a patient needs.

4 When they think an animal may have broken a leg.

5 They run a comb through their fur.

6 By using a thermometer.

7 A drug that puts an animal deeply to sleep before an operation.

8 They rest in a cage at the hospital.

Useful contacts

www.allaboutpets.org.uk
A website that gives pet care tips on dogs, cats, gerbils, rabbits, guinea pigs, hamsters and horses.

www.animalrescuers.co.uk
A website listing organisations that care for rescued wildlife in need of help all around the UK.

www.pdsa.org.uk/youngpdsa
This website includes on-line games, competitions, pet stories and challenges, as well as the address for sending off for a free education pack for teachers.

I love looking after animals and every day is different.

29

Index